In memory of Emma.

Is There Anybody Out There?
Interplanetary Questions for Intelligent Earthlings

Written by Ellen Duthie
Illustrated by Aida Novoa and Carlos Egan (Studio Patten)

Original text © Ellen Duthie, 2022
Illustration © Aida Novoa and Carlos Egan of Studio Patten, 2022
Translation © Ellen Duthie, 2025
Translation rights arranged by Agencia Literaria CBQ

U.S. Edition
Publisher and Creative Director
Ilona Oppenheim

Art Director
Jefferson Quintana

Editorial Director
Lisa McGuinness

Publishing Coordinator
Jessica Faroy

This product is made of FSC®-certified and other controlled material.
Tra Publishing is committed to sustainability in its materials and practices.

Printed and bound in China by Artron Art Co., Ltd.

Title was first published in the United States by Tra Publishing in 2025.

First published in Spain, 2022 by Traje de Lobo, SL,
under the original title *¿Hay alguien ahí?*

No part of this book may be reproduced or transmitted in any
form or by any means (electronic or mechanical, including photocopying,
recording or any information retrieval system) without permission
in writing from the publisher.

ISBN: 978-1-962098-23-6

Tra Publishing
245 NE 37th Street
Miami, FL 33137
trapublishing.com

T tra.publishing

1 2 3 4 5 6 7 8 9 10

CONTENTS

THE DONUT FROM BIBOPIA
Background
Protocol
Certainties Reached

IS THERE ANYBODY OUT THERE?
Bibopian Greetings
What is it like to be a human being?
What is it like to be you?
What is gender for?
How do you know what you know?
How do you humans get along?
And how do you get on with other Earthlings?
Is Earth a good home?
Are you humans nice?
Who's in charge over there?
Why do some human beings have so much, while others have so little?
How does language work on Earth?
On Earth, does two plus two always equal four?
Why do you keep making art?
Have you found the meaning of life?
Bibopian Farewell

THE DONUT FROM BIBOPIA

BACKGROUND

The book you have in your hands is, except for these first few pages, a faithful reproduction of the tome found aboard the extraterrestrial spacecraft that landed a year ago on La Victoria beach, in Cadiz, Spain, and was discovered thanks to the fine sense of smell of a lady's poodle on its morning walk.

Upon the pooch's insistent barking, and despite dogs being banned from the beach in question, the woman went down onto the sand and approached the unidentified object, with equal measures of curiosity and caution. At first sight, she thought it was "sort of like a giant donut", but when she got nearer and at last brought herself to stretch out her arm and give it a light prod with her index finger, she soon found out, somewhat to her disappointment, that it was too hard to even think of attempting a bite.

According to the lady's report, the poodle –whose name we have not been given permission to print in this publication– then proceeded to clamber onto the donut. After briefly disappearing through the hole in the middle, the dog popped up again with an expression of satisfaction on its face, having activated the opening mechanism of the spacecraft. Exactly how this occurred remains a mystery. A deafening sound was followed by three articulated legs suddenly springing from the bottom of the donut and lifting it above sand level, where it had previously remained half-buried.

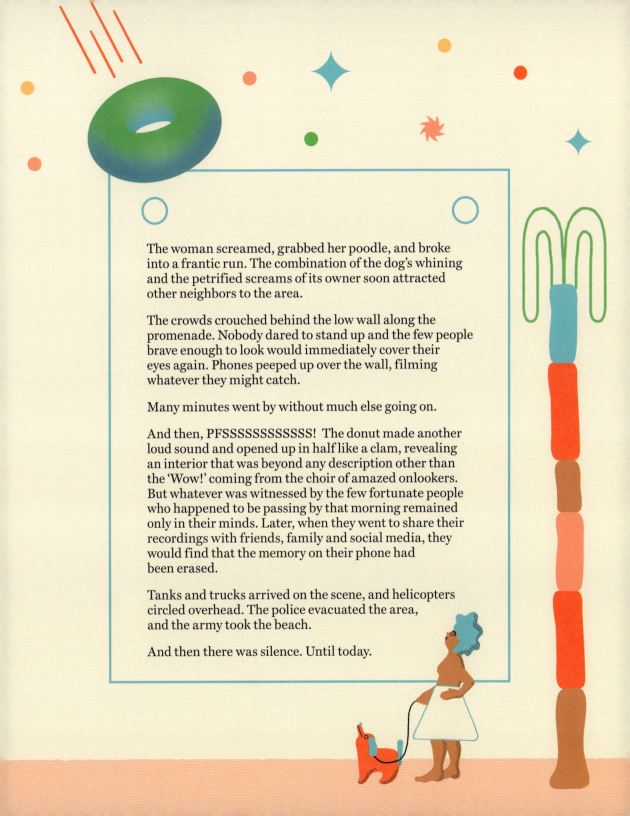

The woman screamed, grabbed her poodle, and broke into a frantic run. The combination of the dog's whining and the petrified screams of its owner soon attracted other neighbors to the area.

The crowds crouched behind the low wall along the promenade. Nobody dared to stand up and the few people brave enough to look would immediately cover their eyes again. Phones peeped up over the wall, filming whatever they might catch.

Many minutes went by without much else going on.

And then, PFSSSSSSSSSSSS! The donut made another loud sound and opened up in half like a clam, revealing an interior that was beyond any description other than the 'Wow!' coming from the choir of amazed onlookers. But whatever was witnessed by the few fortunate people who happened to be passing by that morning remained only in their minds. Later, when they went to share their recordings with friends, family and social media, they would find that the memory on their phone had been erased.

Tanks and trucks arrived on the scene, and helicopters circled overhead. The police evacuated the area, and the army took the beach.

And then there was silence. Until today.

PROTOCOL

In the event of a suspected manifestation of extraterrestrial intelligent life, the Protocol for Post-Detection of Extraterrestrial Intelligence (PPDEI) establishes that, before going public with any information whatsoever regarding said manifestation, a team comprising experts in several disciplines should do everything in their hands to confirm or rule out the suspicion.

Over the last ten months, the members of a multidisciplinary team from the Institute for the Analysis of Extraterrestrial Objects and Messages (IAEOM), established specifically for the inspection of the unidentified flying object landed on the beach of Cadiz, have worked conscientiously on the study and interpretation of the items found inside the donut-shaped vehicle, as well as of the spacecraft itself.

After this first phase of research, despite still being left with many more questions than answers, we are finally in a position to break our silence and confirm four findings, which we share here as a first partial report of certainties reached in the study titled The Donut from Bibopia.

CERTAINTIES REACHED

CERTAINTY NUMBER 1: THE ORIGIN OF THE DONUT FROM BIBOPIA IS NOT TERRESTRIAL.

Our preliminary analyses have allowed us to determine with certainty that the chemical composition of the spacecraft is incompatible with a terrestrial origin. The material of the donut is hard on the outside, as the lady on her morning walk complained, but discombobulatingly vaporous inside, with a set of properties that defy the rules of terrestrial physics in ways that are as revolutionary as endlessly entertaining. In the following months, studies to determine the origin of the spacecraft will continue. Our current working hypothesis is that the materials hail from a planet called Bibopia, the exact location of which remains unknown.

CERTAINTY NUMBER 2: HUMANITY HAS RECEIVED THE FIRST SCIENTIFICALLY VERIFIED EXTRATERRESTRIAL COMMUNICATION.

One of the objects found inside the spacecraft matches the artifact human beings call 'book'*. At first sight and touch, the pages of the book seem to be made of paper, but the properties of the material, impossible to tear and seemingly infinitely stretchable (tested by means of an obstinate experiment performed by 43 members of the team) allow us to confirm with no room whatsoever for any doubt, that the paper's origin is extraterrestrial.

Made up almost in its entirety of questions and titled *Is There Anybody Out There? Interplanetary Questions for Intelligent Earthlings*, the book does indeed constitute the first extraterrestrial message received on Earth to be verified by science.

*Along with this book, three other objects were found inside the Donut from Bibopia. We have as yet been unable to decode or understand any of these three objects in any way or manner, but we will continue to study them until we reach some (any!) kind of certainty.

CERTAINTY NUMBER 3: PLANET EARTH HAS BEEN UNDER EXTRATERRESTRIAL STUDY AND OBSERVATION FOR SOME TIME.

The analysis of the content of the book found in the spacecraft suggests that Bibopians started observing Earth at least three terrestrial centuries ago.

This would lend some credence to the hypothesis known as 'the galactic zoo'. According to this idea, the reason why intelligent extraterrestrial life had not contacted us before might have been that they were watching us, a bit as if Earth was a huge zoo, and that, either we didn't seem particularly interesting to them, or they deemed that it would be impolite and intrusive to make contact with Earth life. In the case at hand, Bibopians explain the reason themselves in their introductory greeting: they were scared to death of us.

We do not yet know what their exact method of observation is but, judging by their knowledge of human languages (there is some indication that they may not only speak English but possibly all the languages spoken on Earth), we are able to conclude that the observation is constant and attentive, and that Bibopian beings are impressively excellent students.

CERTAINTY NUMBER 4: THERE EXISTS AN EXTRATERRESTRIAL INTELLIGENT LIFE THAT IS SURPRISINGLY SIMILAR TO HUMAN LIFE.

With a view to comparing species, we posed the following question to 100,000 human beings of different ages and places of origin: 'What would you ask an intelligent extraterrestrial being?'.

A comparative analysis of the Bibopian questions included in the book found in the spacecraft, on the one hand, and the human questions of the people that took part in our survey on the other hand, pointed to some surprising results.

Despite other indications that suggest interesting differences between Bipobian beings and human beings, we can confirm that the similarities between the two species are stunning in terms of interests, curiosity, and a shared search for the meaning of life.

We hope this reproduction on earthly paper of *Is There Anybody Out There? Interplanetary Questions for Intelligent Earthlings*, prepared by bibopianity specially for humanity, reaches as many human beings as possible. It is an honor and a privilege to share this discovery.

Ellen Duthie, On behalf of the **IAEOM** multidisciplinary team

Is There Anybody Out There?
Interplanetary Questions for Intelligent Earthlings
is the first message sent to humanity from bibopianity.
It has been reproduced in two copies only, one for archiving
and the other for sending, in the Bibopian year 34095
after the Event That Is Never Named.

The book contains a selection of the questions that
Bibopian beings addressed specially to the human beings
of Earth in response to the request from the
CONTACT EARTH project.

Hello! Hello Helloooooo?

IS THERE ANYBODY OUT THERE?

Intelligent life can ask surprisingly unintelligent questions! Of course there is someone out there! Surely it must be someone who is reading these words!

This greeting in the human language English is written by a Bibopian being specialized in human languages:

A BIG HELLO TO HUMANITY

Yes, human beings, there is other intelligent life in the Universe!

No, human beings, no need to panic!

We write in peace, but above all, we write in curiosity.
We have been watching you for some time but had not dared
to establish contact until now.

We Bibopians have many questions, such as the one
that finally made us overcome our fear and send you this first
Bibopian-human communication: What if the main trait
shared by all intelligent lives in the Universe was
a particularly enthusiastic passion for questions?

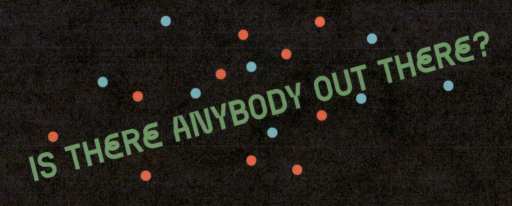

We will listen to your musings
with keen Bibopian interest.

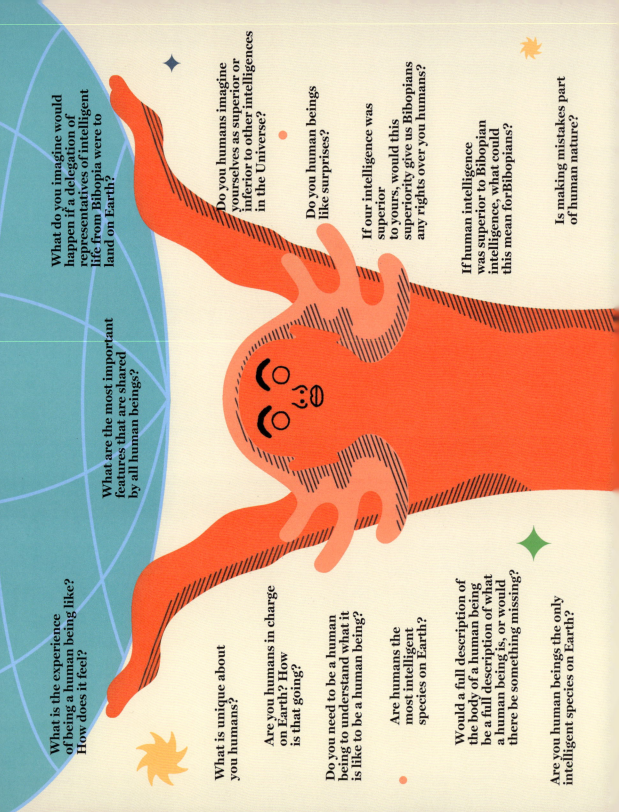

What do you imagine would happen if a delegation of representatives of intelligent life from Bibopia were to land on Earth?

Do you humans imagine yourselves as superior or inferior to other intelligences in the Universe?

Do you human beings like surprises?

If our intelligence was superior to yours, would this superiority give us Bibopians any rights over you humans?

If human intelligence was superior to Bibopian intelligence, what could this mean for Bibopians?

Is making mistakes part of human nature?

What are the most important features that are shared by all human beings?

What is the experience of being a human being like? How does it feel?

What is unique about you humans?

Are you humans in charge on Earth? How is that going?

Do you need to be a human being to understand what it is like to be a human being?

Are humans the most intelligent species on Earth?

Would a full description of the body of a human being be a full description of what a human being is, or would there be something missing?

Are you human beings the only intelligent species on Earth?

WHAT IS IT LIKE TO BE A HUMAN BEING?

Are you humans friendly or aggressive? Are your intentions good or not really?

Does humanity make progress?

If we suggested that the entire population of Bibopia migrate to Earth due to our planet being uninhabitable, how do you think humans would react? Would you be receptive? Would it depend? On what?

Can you imagine a perfect human? Can you provide a description? Could a perfect human exist?

What questions do you have for Bibopians about our experience of being Bibopian?

Is the experience of being a human being the same wherever you live and whatever your resources?

Can a human being be 'inhuman'?

What reasons (if any) do you have to feel proud of being human?

What reasons (if any) do you have to feel ashamed of being human?

If you were all-powerful, would you change anything about humans? What would you change?

Do you think that living beings from other planets should have the same rights as human beings or does it depend? If it depends, what does it depend on?

If you were from another planet, would you let humans in or not? Why?

What do you think of the idea of space tourism? Appealing? Why? Why not?

What do you imagine would happen if a delegation of representatives of intelligent life from Earth were to land on Bibopia?

- Do you think you could be the leader of your planet one day? Why?
- What do other human beings think you are like?
- What groups are you not part of?
- Do you like or dislike the idea of allowing another human being or Bibopian being to become you for a few days?
- Could there be someone else who knew more about you than yourself?
- What groups are you part of?
- What groups would you never ever want to be part of?
- Are you a model human being? Why?
- What do you have that is unique about you that no other human being has?
- Are there any groups you will never get to be part of?
- Is there anything you would rather not know about yourself?
- Would you mind swapping bodies with someone else or are you rather attached to yours?
- Do you think you would be a different 'you' if you had been born in a different family, country, or planet?
- Would you object to the idea of you being cloned for us to take one or several of your clones to Bibopia? Why?
- Would you portray yourself differently if you knew that nobody was going to judge you for it?
- Is it necessary to be 'you' in order to know what it's like to be you, or can you explain it in a way that other beings could understand it?
- What would you ask a Bibopian being about the experience of being that Bibopian being in particular?
- What groups are you not part of, but would like to be part of?
- Are you replaceable? Could a different human being replace you in your life? In what ways could they and in what ways couldn't they? Could a robot replace you? What about a Bibopian?
- If you could 'perfect' yourself, would you choose to? What would you change?

WHAT IS GENDER FOR?

Bibopian beings have no concept of gender. Are we missing out?

What does it feel like to feel like a girl? Or how do you think it feels?

Are there different ways of being a girl?

Do you think it would be a good thing or a bad thing for all human beings to choose the sex of their babies? Why?

What does it feel like to feel like a boy? Or how do you think it feels?

Are there different ways of being a boy?

What differences and what similarities are there between a boy and a girl?

What is a woman?

What is a female human being?

What are the advantages of dividing human beings into genders? Are there any disadvantages?

What differences and what similarities are there between a woman and a man?

What is a man?

What is a male human being?

Can a man be feminine?

What is it that makes you a woman or a man?

If you had the power to create a new species, would you give individuals a gender or not? Why or why not?

Can a woman be masculine?

Would you be a different person if you had been born a different sex? Why or why not? If you think you would be different, in what way?

Are there any advantages or disadvantages to being a man? Are there any advantages or disadvantages to being a woman? What about to being neither a woman nor a man, or to being both?

Is there a midpoint between masculine and feminine?

Besides gender, could you make a list of all (or many of) the things that define the identity of a human being?

What is the difference between the gender and the sex of a human being?

How would your life change if suddenly, overnight, you woke up with a body of the opposite sex? How would your life change immediately? How would it change in the long run?

How important is gender for the life of human beings?

Do people of different genders have a different experience of the world? In what ways do they and in what ways don't they have a different experience?

What would the most masculine being in the Universe be like?

What would the most feminine being in the Universe be like?

Do you human beings have to be either female or male? Is it possible to be both at once? Or neither?

Is it possible to learn to be a girl or a boy?

Do you have any interesting questions about the Bibopian experience of genderless existence?

- What difference is there between believing something and knowing something?
- Would it be a good thing to know it all?
- Are there any other species on Earth with the ability to gain knowledge?
- Do all human beings have access to the same knowledge? If you don't think so, what does access to knowledge depend on for human beings?
- Can you distinguish between reality and dream? Always? How?
- When it comes to the unknown, are you more fearful or more curious?
- Do you have enough interests, or would you like to have more? Why?
- Does human knowledge have limitations? If you think so, what limitations?
- Are your senses reliable?
- If you human beings were to discover that you are part of an experiment devised by superior beings that are watching you with curiosity, how would it affect you? Would you go on with your life as usual? Would you try to do something about it? What?
- What is imagination for?
- Can you human beings see the future?
- How do the thoughts of human beings come about?
- What would you like to learn how to do?
- What is it like to have two eyes only?
- Are human beings born intelligent or do they become intelligent over time?
- What are you dying to know?
- In what different ways do you human beings gain knowledge about the world?
- Do your senses show you the external world as it is in reality? How do you know?
- What are the most important questions and answers in life?
- Are you human beings always thinking, or can you pause your thoughts in any way?

HOW DO YOU KNOW WHAT YOU KNOW?

- In this book, did we represent humans in the correct color? How can you tell?
- Do you think we Bibopians exist? Why?
- Do you have any questions about Bibopian senses and our knowledge of the world?
- Is human science capable of explaining everything? Will it ever be?
- Do you think it will ever be possible to build an artificial being capable of thinking in a way that is indistinguishable from the way a natural human being thinks?
- If you human beings don't know something, what can you do about it?
- Are there any things that you human beings know with absolute certainty? What?
- Do telescopes show things more like they 'really' are than your eyes?
- Is the human brain and the human mind the same thing?
- Does your knowledge belong to you, or would you be prepared to share it? Would you want anything in exchange for it, or would you share it out of generosity?
- What do you feel is the most important thing to learn about in life?
- What do you human beings do with your knowledge?
- Can you think of an example of something you believe but cannot prove? What makes you believe it?

HOW DO YOU HUMANS GET ALONG?

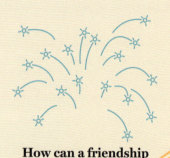

What is friendship?

How can a friendship be broken?

In what sense are all you human beings equal? In what sense are you human beings different from one another?

What is it like to have a best friend?

What are the features of a good friend?

Are all human beings born free and equal in dignity and rights?

Is a friend different from a good friend? What is the difference? And what about the difference between a friend and an acquaintance?

Relationships between Bibopians are not based on love but rather on biological compatibility. What is love, exactly?

What do you love? And who do you love?

Can you human beings have friendships with dogs? With robots? With Bibopians?

Are human beings a united front?

What would the perfect friend be like?

What do you human beings need in order to live in peace?

Does friendship have any rules?

Is peace the absence of war or is it something more than that?

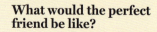
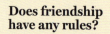

What would you be prepared to fight for?

Is there anybody you would fight for?

Are some human lives more valuable than others, or are all lives equally valuable?

Is killing human beings justifiable under any circumstances?

What causes wars among human beings?

Does war have any rules?

Would you fight for your country against another country?

Is violence part of human nature?

Would you fight for your planet against another planet?

Are human nature and war related in any way?

Are there any necessary wars?

Do you hate anything or anyone?

What is the difference between a just war and an unjust war?

Is there anything you could never ever forgive?

Can war ever be a necessary means to achieve peace?

Who is more important, you or your neighbor?

What conditions would have to be met for you human beings to stop engaging in war?

If a loved one died, but had had an identical copy made of them, would you still love the copy the same as the original?

In war, does anything go?

Do you have any questions about how we Bibopians get along?

AND HOW DO YOU GET ON WITH OTHER EARTHLINGS?

Do you have any interesting questions regarding how we Bibopians get along with other species living on Bibopia?

Is the life of some Earthlings more important than that of others? How do you measure the importance of a given life?

Would you think it was acceptable for Bibopians to adopt humans as pets? What advantages and what disadvantages do you think being pets would bring you?

Are you human beings the most important Earthlings for the Universe? Why?

Do viruses have a right to live?

What special qualities allow you humans to dominate the other species on your planet?

Which species of Earthlings do human beings eat? Why do you eat some of them but not others?

Why do you human beings think it is acceptable to keep other Earthlings as pets? Why is it acceptable to keep some animals as pets, but not others?

Could Bibopians become Earthlings?

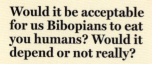

Would it be acceptable for us Bibopians to eat you humans? Would it depend or not really?

Should any human being have the right to keep a pet, or should they fulfil a set of requirements in order to keep one?

What would we Bibopians need to have in order for you to consider us to be 'persons'?

Do you think there are any cases in which it might be justified to use animals in scientific experiments? What about using human beings? What about using beings from another planet?

Would it be acceptable for Bibopians to test our medical treatments on human beings? Would it depend or not really?

On planet Earth, is cruelty towards other Earthlings as frowned upon as cruelty towards other human beings? Why? What is the difference?

Besides human beings, are there any other Earthling species that might be considered 'persons' of sorts?

Do you humans eat your pets? Why?

Do all lives on Earth have value in themselves?

Do any other Earthling species have dignity or is it only applicable to human beings? Why?

Is it justifiable to test medicine on other species before using it on human beings?

If a human being had to choose between saving another human and saving an animal, which would they save and why?

What life on Earth is least valuable for human beings? What is such a low ranking based on?

Are there ever any circumstances in which the killing of non-human living beings (such as ants, rats or other species) might be justified?

IS EARTH A GOOD HOME?

From your human point of view, is cutting down a tree more or less abhorrent than killing a rat? Why?

Is planet Earth a better home for some species than for others?

Who does the Earth belong to? Does it not belong to anyone, or does it belong to everyone?

One thousand years ago, do you think planet Earth was a better or a worse home than it is today?

In one thousand years' time, do you think planet Earth will be a better or a worse home than it is today?

Is planet Earth a better home for some human beings than for others?

Would planet Earth be less valuable without human beings?

Do you think planet Earth might be a good home for Bibopian beings? Why?

Is planet Earth valuable in itself? Or is it only valuable because of the life on it?

Is planet Earth welcoming?

Do you think that the pollution of planet Earth is a problem because of how it might affect human beings, or is it a problem because the environment is valuable in itself? Why would it have value in itself? What would give it its value?

Would it be better or worse for the Earth if human beings were to become extinct?

Does humanity have a plan in place to fight the climate change that is affecting planet Earth?

On planet Earth, does nature have rights? Does the sea have rights? What about rivers? Or do only animals have rights? Why?

What is the place of human beings within nature on planet Earth?

Are you human beings to blame for the state of planet Earth? Are you responsible? What is the difference?

Do you have any plans to explore other planets with a view to moving there?

If you could design a better planet, how would you design it?

What makes a place a good home? What requirements must it meet?

Are you humans good tenants? What are the terms of the agreement for you to live on planet Earth?

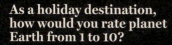

As a holiday destination, how would you rate planet Earth from 1 to 10?

Are you humans part of Earth's nature or are you users of Earth's nature?

Would any place on Earth be a good holiday destination or are some better than others? Which would you recommend?

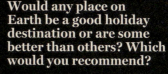

What responsibilities do intelligent beings of a planet have towards the environment of that planet? Why do we have those responsibilities? Where does the responsibility arise from?

Do you have any questions about what Bibopia is like as a home?

ARE YOU HUMANS NICE?

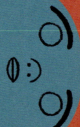

If evil did not exist, would good exist?

What would you do differently if you knew that nobody was going to condemn (or praise) your behavior?

Is there a limit to how good a human can be? Who do you think may have come closest to the limit? Are you close? Would you like to be?

Does humanity have a promising plan to do away with cruelty?

If good did not exist, would evil exist?

Would you sometimes like to behave 'worse' than you behave? Why? And what's stopping you?

What is the best thing you would be capable of doing?

Do you think that if you lived forever, you'd become a better or a worse human being?

Are you a good person? Could you be better? How?

Would you be capable of accepting a bribe for doing something you think is wrong? What would it depend on? Can you think of an interesting example that would make it hard to decide?

What is the worst thing you would be capable of doing?

Would you sometimes like to behave 'better' than you behave? Why? And what's stopping you?

Are you trustworthy?

Would there be good and evil on Earth if there were no human beings?

Does the end justify the means?

Two people, one you know, the other a stranger, need urgent help. If you can only help one of them, how would you decide who to help?

Is it pleasurable to behave well?

Do you have any questions for us Bibopians? Are you concerned about our intentions?

Can you be a good human and do (some) bad things? How many bad things would be too many?

How important is it for you humans to tell the truth?

How can a bad human being become a good human being? And how can a good one become a bad one?

What is it exactly to behave well?

How do you know what the right thing to do is?

Are some humans good and other humans bad? Why?

Is it pleasurable to behave badly?

What do you think is worse, to intend to do good and do harm without meaning to, or to intend to do evil and fail in the attempt?

How many of your ideas of what is right and what is wrong have you accepted without thinking about them too much?

- Who does your country belong to?
- What are human prisons for? What is the difference between prisons and zoos?
- What limits, if any, should there be to the freedom of human beings?
- What kind of human being do you think should have access to power?
- Do you think it is inevitable for there to be inequalities among human beings or do you think there might be a way to get rid of inequality?
- What is more important, freedom or security?
- Would it be desirable for no humans to have any power over any other humans?
- What are governments for? Could humans live without government?
- Do you human beings obey the law because you have to, or because you want to?
- Who decides who is in charge in countries on Earth? What about on Earth as a whole?
- Why are there more male leaders than female leaders on Earth?
- Do all human beings deserve equal rights?
- If we arrived on Earth and asked you to take us to your leader, who would you take us to?
- What kind of training and traits should a human being have if they wish to become a leader?
- If there is a rule or law that is unfair, what can you do about it?
- On planet Earth, does power always lead to corruption?
- Could you human beings live without being in society?
- What rights do you have? Why do you have those rights? What is it that gives you those rights?

WHO'S IN CHARGE OVER THERE?

- Do children take part in important decisions? Why?
- If you were in charge, would you allow extraterrestrial species to come to planet Earth? Why?
- If you were in charge, would you limit technological development in any way, or not?
- Any interesting questions about who is in charge in Bibopia?

- What responsibilities would you have if you had been born one hundred Earth years ago? What has made those responsibilities change over time?
- If you were in charge of a democratic state, from what age would you allow humans to vote?
- What are your responsibilities? Why do you have those responsibilities?
- In human societies, how do you respond to rebellion?
- If you were in charge, would you protect other human beings from certain information for their own good?

- What rights do you enjoy today that you would not have enjoyed if you had been born one hundred Earth years ago? What has made those rights change over time?
- Are there any situations in which rebellion is justified?
- What goals do you think all governments of all countries on Earth should have?
- If you were in charge, would you choose democracy as a system of government? Why?

WHY DO SOME HUMAN BEINGS HAVE SO MUCH, WHILE OTHERS HAVE SO LITTLE?

In Bibopia, we have no private property. Are we missing out?

Are there any human beings that don't have anything at all?

What belongs to you? Do you need more? Would you like more?

Is your life yours? If it is yours, what rights does it come with?

Is there any other human that belongs to you?

Is your body yours? If it is yours, does that mean you can do absolutely whatever you want with it?

Do you belong to your family?

Does your family belong to you?

Are there any things that should belong to everyone? What things? Does 'everyone' include the entire Universe?

How many of the ideas that you have are yours?

Is there anything in your life that you could never give away? Why is it so important to you?

Is it possible to have too much? How much would be just right to have?

Are there some things that shouldn't belong to anyone? What things?

It would seem that the more humans care about belongings, the harder it is for them when they lose them. Would it be better if stuff didn't matter to us?

Is money valuable in itself?

Is money more than a piece of paper? What gives money its value?

What would planet Earth be like without money?

What does money represent?

Can money be dangerous?

Would planet Earth be better or worse off if human beings did not own anything? What advantages do you think there would be in doing away with all private property? What disadvantages can you think of?

How many different ways can something become 'yours'?

How many different ways could something stop being 'yours'?

Who does the sky belong to? Who do the seas belong to?

How could the resources of a country be distributed fairly? What about the resources of planet Earth? What about the resources of the Universe?

Do you think there should be a limit to the amount of money a human being can own? If you think so, what should the limit be? And who should calculate it?

Who does planet Earth belong to?

For a human to have something, should they deserve it? Why?

Who deserves what?

For a human, what does it mean to 'have it all'?

What is private property for?

Is there anything that belongs to you right now that it is impossible for you to ever lose?

In Bibopia we don't have any money. Are we missing out on something?

What is money for?

Do you think there should be a limit of belongings per human being? If you think so, what should the limit be? And who should calculate it?

It seems that humans often inherit money and personal things from their parents or loved ones. Do you think that's fair or unfair?

We Bibopians don't have any shopping experience whatsoever. Is it an experience that brings happiness?

HOW DOES LANGUAGE WORK ON EARTH?

- Are you human beings born with language, or do you develop it over time?
- Are there any things for which there are no human words?
- What happens if a human being decides to ignore the rules of language?
- Does language shape your thoughts or is it the other way around, do your thoughts shape your language?
- What is the relationship between language and the world on planet Earth?
- How do speakers of a human language reach an agreement about what words mean?
- Could you human beings understand the world without language?
- Are there any other Earthlings that have language?
- Is communication between species possible on Earth?
- For human beings, is it possible to think without words?
- Are there any things that it is better not to say?
- If a Bibopian were to repeat all the sounds of a human being, would they be speaking the language of that human being?
- Could there be a language that only one individual understood?
- For human beings, is it possible to think something that cannot be expressed in words?
- Must language always make sense?
- How does language get its meaning?
- Can a language continue to exist even if no one speaks it?

- On planet Earth, do words have power?
- Does language give some humans power over other humans?
- Can language change human thought? Can it change human behavior?
- Can language make the world better? Can language harm the world?
- Should freedom of speech have any limitations or not?
- Do you humans think differently depending on the language you speak?
- Are thoughts sentences unsaid? Are all human thoughts made up of words? If not, what of?
- What are metaphors for? When do human beings choose to express something with a metaphor rather than with a literal description? What benefits do metaphors offer?
- Why do you humans tell stories?
- How does irony work? How are we to know whether to take something ironically or literally?
- In your language, are all statements necessarily either true or false or can you think of any exceptions?
- Do you have any questions about Bibopian language?
- What words would you welcome a Bibopian with if they turned up on your doorstep?
- Are you humans good at learning languages?
- What would the human world be like without language?
- Are there any cases where 'no' means 'yes'?
- What do you humans use language for?
- Are there any cases where 'yes' means 'no'?

ON EARTH, DOES TWO PLUS TWO ALWAYS EQUAL FOUR?

How many even numbers exist? How many odd numbers exist? And how many numbers are there in total? If the answer to these three questions is the same, how can that be?

Would human mathematical truths exist if nobody thought of them?

Do you think there might be a world where two plus two does not actually equal four?

Was your mathematics invented or discovered?

What is greater, infinity or double infinity?

Is this triangle possible?

Do you think there could be a kind of mathematics that is illogical?

Are there any differences between human numbers and the symbols for human numbers?

Is mathematics a language?

If you subtract infinity from infinity, is the answer also infinity? Which of the two infinities do you have left and what is the difference between them?

Are numbers ideas?

What is mathematics used for on Earth?

Do you think it is possible that some day you might discover that all human numbers are wrong?

If we Bibopians had, for instance, a total of 12 fingers across 4 hands, how would a human and a Bibopian hold hands?

How many different things can counting be useful for?

Is it possible to imagine an infinite Universe without imagining an infinite time?

Could there be another mathematics with rules that are different from the mathematics you have on Earth?

Do you think there could be geometric figures as yet unknown to human beings? How might you go about discovering them?

Is the statement 'Everything we Bibopians write is false' true or false?

Is infinity a number? In what sense is it a number and in what sense isn't it a number?

Does time have a beginning?

How can you humans be so sure that your mathematics is true?

Is mathematics an art? Why?

Are numbers real? Do they exist outside the minds that think them?

How does mathematics help you understand your world?

Could time have an end?

WHY DO YOU KEEP MAKING ART?

What exactly do you humans call 'art?'

What do music, poetry, literature, cinema, dance, theatre, painting and sculpture have in common for human beings to place them within the same category of 'art?'

How important is art in the education of human beings?

Why do human beings create art?

How can Bibopians understand what is art and what is not art?

What is art for?

Can art be bad or is it no longer art if it is bad?

Are all human beings capable of creating artworks or only some?

Is there anything that all human beings on Earth would agree is ugly?

Is art always beautiful or can there be ugly art?

Are there any other Earthlings capable of making art, besides human beings?

Is it possible to learn to distinguish what is beautiful from what is ugly? How?

What makes one artwork better than another?

Is there anything that all human beings on Earth would agree is beautiful?

Is beauty a matter of opinion or are there things that are beautiful even though there may be some humans who do not see them as such?

What do beautiful things have in common for human beings to consider them beautiful?

Is a copy of a work of art also a work of art? Which is more valuable, the copy or the original? Why?

If one human being thinks something is art and another thinks it is not art, is one of the two wrong?

Is there a relationship between art and knowledge?

Can a mathematical problem be beautiful?

Can a stone be art?

What is beauty?

Would it make sense to take a vote on the beauty or ugliness of something?

Who decides what is art and what is not art?

Can a bad human being make a good work of art?

Is art a waste of time? Are there more important things than art?

Can an artwork be liked by someone who doesn't understand it?

What factors influence the value of artworks?

In Bibopia we gave up doing art many millennia ago (the illustrations for this book are our first artistic expression in around 10,000 Earth years). What advantages do you think there would be if we were to start creating art again?

Is it possible for something that is an artwork at a given time to cease being an artwork at a later date? How?

Does the life of a human being have more meaning than the life of a rat? Does it have more meaning than the life of all rats on Earth?

If human beings never died, would your lives have more, or less meaning?

For a life to have meaning, does it need a purpose or goal?

What would our Bibopian lives have to be like for humans to consider that they have meaning?

Does the discovery, upon reading this book, that you are not the only intelligent beings in the Universe, change the meaning of human life in any interesting way?

What is the meaning of the life of a gorilla living in a zoo on Earth? What is the meaning of the life of a gorilla living in a forest on Earth?

Do some human lives have more meaning than others?

What might bring motivation to human beings if you lived forever?

If you humans were to discover that the life you are living is really an experiment where planet Earth is a huge zoo run by extraterrestrials who observe humans for entertainment purposes, would your lives have less meaning, more meaning, or the same meaning? Why?

What would you like there to remain of you after you die?

What things are you dying to experience in your life?

What things do you do that make you lose track of time? When you lose track of time, is it a sign that you are enjoying what you are doing?

Is there a difference between living and existing?

HAVE YOU FOUND THE MEANING OF LIFE?

Do you think pain and sorrow should be avoided at all costs?

Would a life with no moments of suffering be more, or less, satisfactory than a life with some moments of suffering? Which of the two lives would have more meaning?

What things bring you sadness in your life?

Are there cases in which suffering can be enjoyable for human beings?

What makes you cry?

Can pain and suffering ever be good?

Is seeking happiness and escaping unhappiness enough to bring meaning to life?

If there was no suffering on Earth, would the life of human beings have more meaning?

Is it possible to have too much enjoyment?

Is the most important purpose in life to be happy? Or might there be a more important or equally important purpose?

Can you imagine a life of happiness without laughter?

What brings you happiness in life?

What makes you excited?

What are the most important things in your life?

Do you have any questions about how we Bibopians go about searching for the meaning of life?

Can the meaning of life be transmitted? If you communicate the meaning of life to someone, would it be enough for their life to acquire meaning?

HELLO? ARE YOU STILL THERE?

THANK YOU VERY MUCH, HUMAN.

You have been very, very
interesting in your reading
and in your thought.

BIBOPIANITY IS SHY,
BUT WE WILL STAY IN TOUCH.

Notice: Any suspicion that this book may be science fiction shall be interpreted as a sign of intelligent life on the other side of the page.